NOW LAYS

Now Lays
The Sunshine By

Andrew Hughes

BookThug | Toronto | 2010

LIBRARY AND ARCHIVES CANADA
CATALOGUING IN PUBLICATION

Hughes, Andrew, 1975-
    Now lays the sunshine by / Andrew Hughes. -- 1st ed.

Poems. ISBN 978-1-897388-58-7

    I. Title.

PS3608.U328N68 2010   811'.6   C2010-902125-8

*"A force gathers that will cry loudlier
than the most metal music, loudlier,
like an instinctive incantation."*

Wallace Stevens, *Dutch Graves
in Bucks County*

TABLE OF CONTENTS

HESSIAN DECIBELS

For Nora Rose—my jive
turkey—
w/
love
  always

THE NEW WAVE OF AMERICAN HEAVY METAL

For Russell Dillon

wé fúckt úp
  & we hate you
    for making us admit it

 but you were
a shining example
  of honest songwriting
    that night
        together   alone
       onstage in
    the Grand Ballroom

      & what you thought
      were dreams

     just rags we used
       to stop the bleeding

CLOUDS & COMPLICATED HALOS

SOUND YEARS

my derelict Atlantic
lily of my wild perdition
let's compare jerkwaters
who'll flinch first
post-hick & lyrical
notebook fatigued on
first person dissonant
pink clouds & country roads
my noise jones
talcumed into bluets

SO THIS IS WHAT IT MUST FEEL LIKE TO SMILE

all our life we've associated
dark clouds w/ rain
whimsical young stargazers
on nu-metal whiskey
tours royalty beneath
the lemon trees
Villa America days
if we were to watch
something what would we watch

BUSHWICK VESPERS

sorry to be a prick
forgot it's morning by you
my favorite sweet
slow golden hit
start spinning
in yr undulating twill
skirt just below the knee
the weather
left me forgetful
armageddon week phone sale
these last remaining survivors
could be yrs

GO MORNING

prop up the clouds
that may be lowering
everything January
must go I read
yr wall today oh boy
weird the expectation
as it seemed to us
lay me down one time more
haven't seen you in forever

LAST OUTLAWS

w/ the latest developments
in college rock
the time of the year
men in the village grew their beards
maybe you're still a puddle
something bright at work here
at night I turn my ringer off
talk to me about ghosts
she was asking after you then

VICTORY ODE

dive bar guitars
bluebird the alt. clouds
memory wire
horror down cupid's avarice
first balladeer's avoider
dandruff snuff we're
some pussies
are prettier than others
courtship antagonism
another American after hours
birdwatcher coda squandered
in paraphrase
o winsome phenomenal pentecost
  o loud around the wood
    a voice in empty room echoes
      does not very well abide

NOW LAYS THE SUNSHINE BY

mini zen garden
white sand instructions
alt. clouds birds flowers
averaging out the average
angling degrees
way the body
attempts to correct itself
when it falls
come here to me now
everything must go
the one the other will absorb
invisible solid
living corduroy tattle
sorry to be a prick
we fight because we can
my fucking heartsong

VEXATION NOTCH

Flutter & blushful, western manic leafy beats,
assert the laud to loop & lope, a yurt
fit for a lecturer, wastrel swami flares
sleepy yups, roll-bounce in rinks
guilt blazes on, time to lime the lilacs,
matin skippers, the bangles of balsams
say eerily the esprit of whom?
Flange doesn't rhyme w/vibrate.
Alone & dapper takes a sip & rips it up
tips the, mountains of, super new
happiness in the text an intimation of
the bagatelles of September
for endless games of June.
In the brazen glow of artifical lights,
we should be golden.

ALT. CLOUDS

nothing mere about you
still the saddest nights
super magic smoke clouds life-like
trick pencil set
apart from your glaze
footloose rejoice
squirting pen hot
pepper chewing gum
fake dogshit hand buzzer
if we were but to fasten our attention
as any on TV or
movies attention Virginia
if you're traveling this summer
the balloon expands
move farther apart to make room
best divide the crickets
dig my anharmonicity
sunshine eyeburst
makeup kit radio
control turbo leopard archery set
we fight because we can

THRASHIN LYRE

rhapsodic & homesick spectator
checkpoint carnation roll off decision dice
October wrapt in cooler vegetation
old hat chromed British menu thru
Sunday swears a satanic outlay
more melodic rubbish trips glam
in great style rhinestone
of Cambridge thunders
feels explained expelled vivrant
buried worry in the middle of last
thank you for the mushroom
beats the elf of mountains
low pressure vampire
to the clear small drop of rain
for awe citizens look
to monument to sting peroxide's
the why of quiet
wooden looks ahead
yankee cries Moose Skowron
by soothsayer memory pulls
crucial swells up fickle
beside a body water song
w/ blue filled at loiters
this climate that
crimps where you want
a phantom some would be

& THE GOLD OF THEIR BODIES
(BRETON GIRLS BY THE SEA)

empty coffee can strung

from flagpole clanks

in wind

the voltage stencil of yr hummingbird

vertigo a colorful about brought

one of many stunning features

of my landscape

while golden Breton girls by the sea

go spinal

go nipples up

in the cathedral

& another bacteria Saturday

when the evening sun go down

PURE COUNTRY

the best book of spaceships
kept me up all night
those first one thousand winters
an aspect of childhood &
a blast pattern
lost in the glass between days
                    ghostlonesome
w/ snowforce
it's yr first kiss Charlie
Brown & scale calls
into question so many things
what would I do w/o
the geese to mark the seasons

isn't it beautiful
the black hole at the center of every galaxy

POCKET GUIDES LANDSCAPE

on the river the healing continues
in due season make the sunshine come
the bloomers made me decide
to leave the revolution in the night
no surge no answer
thanks for letting me snow
ghostriding the Devil's Whip
who knows where the day will take us
the strange unmade my head broke me up w/

BRIGHT GOT HEAVY IN THE STREET

"...*Mr Heartbreak, the New Man,*
come to farm a crazy land..."

John Berryman, *Dream Song 5*

EASTERN STANDARD

goldfish around her bed while she dreams.
Something amazing, a boy falling out of the sky,

I am the moon's lost ember, unearthly pallor.
The truth is, when you're alone your bed is smaller,

One time we tried crushing our Zoloft up and doing lines
to each a pile of dirt; a Letter; My dear fuckers,

Girls who read Virginia Woolf glisten
Mild effects are the result.

That mind obedient to disorder ruins roundly,
I hate what I am and I hate what I am not.

I would have hummed to the statue
Or Aristotle's skeleton. Let him hang out

Where angels turned into honeysuckle & poured nectar into my mouth
while I thought of nothing but its darkness

and for years I believed
a dog with a rotten tongue hesitates to lick the sick man.

strangely her features are Easter
Like Schoenberg's unplayable String Trio

I found a decade of poetry dead.
All leave is cancelled to⁄night: we must say good⁄bye.

All the bang⁄about worlds we knew
Are the eye grown larger, more intense.

I'm Audubon: with an ink for the injured bird I carry around inside.
Tender feather, tell me a flight thing, never a trap thing, never a fall.

If you stay, the walls will admit their cracks.
There is something fearful in these summer nights that go on forever...

I have turned the camera toward the chamber of overdoses.
With a quiet as old as habit, or the worn sky

Together we lie in the lawns of retardation.
God is a tiger, so people worship him from the trees.

In the old days I had too much respect for nature.
And we wear exhaustion like a painted robe

Love made him weep his pints like you and me.
People threw stones at him, and he ate them.

I've hid in rocks.   Fed by hyenas, vultures, the despised
But another, more urgent question imposes itself—that of poverty.

You say that you are concerned that I drink too much without you,
What I fear most are ordinary things:

just to read Keats letters, drink a beer,
get really dark, richly dark, like

a manifesto on the irregularity of scars.
I walk these hills wearing an Easter dress.

Me and you, we're such punks. Situationalists ready to ride
Far, far beyond the putative canzones

toward your wrist, toward this restaurant nearing closing time: the wine,
I thought: why me, why her & I knew it wouldn't last.

I had stopped believing there were other "I's" when we met,
And the rose sighs Touch me, I am dying

You are my calm world. This is my happiness. To stand, go forward into it.
God bless the occasional terry⁄cloth head⁄band.

This is the dragon's day, the devourer's:
Someone has written Fuck You in empty beer cans

"and doesn't your penis look funny today?" I jacked "off."
Deprived of water, he dies; the rest is mystery.

Your body is the country I'll never return to.
In life I was heroic at times, at

issuing small commands
I was the youngest hero of the iceberg wards.

                    Soon the violent rain,
people leap from burning buildings

Death is the mother of beauty, mystical,
The way a bird eats a berry. It resists abrupt ruptures, the perfidious

She had packed up everything left uncharred.
"I am a woman of pleasure" & give back

The red and gold Persian carpet from California.
She who cuts her hands off must drink with her tongue.

Keats wanted the inscription to be
We say God and the imagination are one...

You are the town and we are the clock.
This is the story of how I came to find myself unlovable

I am lonely most of the time, and tired of love.
I once slept with an injured stewardess.

In the song of my anger there is an egg,
and I say I raise my glass to the lovers on the bridge.

And in spring the mad caroling continues long after daylight
It was Easter Monday,

At times, your disinterestedness may seem insincere, to strangers.
When the sun was a child's breath above the Earth

where no dogs howl at the jackhammering lovers
where I never cried

MORNING SPAN

I'll call on you between rains
whenever minutes &
        a monster hit
       matinee landscapes my psalter dumb
you who are so white I could snort you
                on the lamb in Dracula City
& in swims
          stay tuned

a bold timeout for the quarter
        followed by an all new lost
          the country weird going straight
     to blue ray winethick mindnoise preface
              O forgotten Manhattan I'll do
the dirty reggae   w/ you   lyrical but
                different
            asked to leave the amnesia study

at the lavenderfaint birth of this new aria
barefoot but clearheaded

                  raindrop hung off barbedwire
            I'm all good w/ that   for now
                       soon the winter finches will leave
              what a gas
            thought if I ignored it it would go away
fire trucks   a parade

bright got heavy in the street

                    sunclobbered aftereffect casebook

                        on the new deliriants

            spumoni sky duskt

        the spooky rumpus in her pants as I

                    unacquainted wonderfuls unbound

          throttle the lyre electric now

                  play the music that made John Peel cry

                as actors we look to the sky

        to remember our lines

          sweet apple tree past yr eyes

                  sing new Brooklyn Sutras

                  blackout dates

O forgotten Manhattan   O the country weird   if we get separated meet me

on the platform at Union Square

  the suspense of amorous reprise

another allergy spring   nosebleed
aimlessness the new hip
all tweeded up in boutique weed
another post thrash death trip
who knew she'd leave
you weak-kneed   in the lips
but I'm always leaving I've
got a long ways   yet to drive

asked to leave the amnesia study
after another failed attempt
to jump through the hoop of flames
                    my heart healthy enough to fuck
        May's clear alarm
wet in yr sparrowgrace
vibrating boundaries may occur when opposing colors are brought together
a crash of feedback to close the set

the forcefulness of our prayers yielded
great rewards
                    the ban on tritones

                                        lifted

                soon summer nerves
        stalk me along darkled streets
walking w/ my sweet
                beneath the hermaphroditic elms perfect leaves

so the jackstraw   marquee clonks aglow
          long yellow school bus goes by
awake w/
yr laidback
    redneck feedback
    promise me you won't sing
       just close your eyes & floor it
          look for me choir my lips

only no sound I can't write

but I can ride a train &

naturally cranberry meet me between the big rains &

whenever minutes

those spring peepers

dubplate thicks up

April late dark

half-smoked cigarette butt flattened

on platform

the pansies are fine thank you for asking

the sun is shining   roses going still

a blue truck tools by   w/ a white cap

push to talk

the eye of God 450 light years away

that's what they say anyway, the people who study

the sky

barefoot but clearheaded

you who are so white I could snort you

at work in the weather

some compelling horsepower

supple uproar of sprawl

moth atmospheric

the consonantal nonetheless

my cowslip enchantress

rally cap faithful chant back

opposing teams surge

yr tropicana skyline so glam metal
that it may well have been some noble song
the robin's cheerful warble or
the wood thrush's more glorious chant
among the branches in the cool of the day heard
that inspired the Psalmist's poetic utterance
so sensitive to every natural beauty
to the music that made John Peel cry

wuz it Theocritus who sd
you can tell a lot
about a man
by what he considers
psychedelic

in my arcadia there will be no birds
hello/hello/it's me/over
I'm stuck in the star chamber untenured
eating leftovers & drinking screwdrivers
fire trucks   parades   I unstirred
the country weird   hangovers & layovers
in the motel last night I watched Marie-Antoinette
undress   a crash of feedback ends the set

put your hands in the air

to humiliate love remember nothing

a white kitchen   yellow   a vase of flowers   a bowl of star fruit

once the darkness
is announced
              the banquet will begin

HESSIAN DECIBELS

"in
    music's
least melody
    there's

a memory
    it's beginning's
a flowering
    of light"

Frank Samperi, *Of Light*

TOWNIE

Absolute in the cackle battery, a dharma⁄
Feel only serves to embolden
& so emboldened by this grim⁄intimate
Hypothesis, having only jabber – wisps –
Yr kittenish onus *totally on melt*
…in the nerd⁄parallels our revisionism
Quickens w/ sacrifice; undaunted
The adventurers mark X as a position
Like wink, zone, yen. What orchards
There are now are all in apple. Another
Baffled cadenza.

Ordinarily yr psalmody is quite rustic.
We segued into kegger⁄law; the massive
Nobble over the trumpets dark uncertainty
& vastitude, the gathering Hesperian
Worry. Imaginary, jackass. The acquittal
Bests for consonance, because in March
You didn't believe this could happen.

SUNSET POLISH

calling planet dangerous hands
around a high gold year
on the leaves a sudden easy
minor northern radio method
window music
of difference
grey wonders aware
electricity frightens
poem in the middle pollution
child of afternoon flowers
whispered equipment
of all possible hearts
eventually to understand the May design
into movement cotton deep
each confederate longplayer wreathed
butterflies before allocution
these messy do-overs
so beasty & downstream
the pretense of tears begets
erasures of an interim
meandering& so awespired
in the flagship noise
of after-school specials

dog wet tennis ball
sunglared hardwood hallway

dismayed by maybe
　　those toasts shattered

bothersome heartbeat/don't remember

ELECTRIC MILES

Come to call the sunshine, lose
yr flowers in the roar. Leaves
in their new green beckon. Once
again to meet the spring w/
winter curls down my neck. Thrown
to the doves on a cooling
carpet of pine. Point the bell

down. Patrón, anyone? Bright
chromatic sincerity.
Drum up the courage, step o'
ver the puddle. Dear L Train,
at the height of summer yr
paradise is closed. Sulked all
the way back from the meadows.

Turn on the bubble machine.
Turn it up or down but dance.
In the cloud that supports you.
Talk away death. Mystical
village. Math rock sky, I'll be.
Gorgeous in yr glitchery.
Turn it up or down but dance.

One distant day. Electric,
    miles. Growth, as we've known it
is no longer possible.
    Go back to the boom. Dip, shift.
  Sport, twerp. Get wet. We control
the vertical, we control
    the horizontal. Punch out.

Remember what the forest
gave us? You are not like the other
dreamers, if I remember
correctly. Heart-shakened, you
said Indian Summer last
year was a wash. Dis. Stressed. Pressed for
details. Foliage crashed fast.

The promise not to stop. 'Cause
once you start it's hard to. Full
of wonders, sometimes tender.
Tender perennial, push.
Bring a new ache to the green
world, so the eagles of Zeus seem
an extravagant mercy.

Touching instructions. Fables,
   bluer. Suppose an absence.
When the battery goes out
it's time to stop reading. Right
off the line. Got a folksong
   in my heart & hope to die.
Pear, w/ plum bruise. Kites.

Disco above the city.
      Yr dark pastoral, pyrrhic.
      Yr sharp edges chronically
blunted by worry. Chime on!
            "Spiral" out of control. I
         think of you, picking my nose.
               Shift, dip. Get stepping. Disco.

            Above the city, but not
            above the clouds. Below the
            clouds, but above the city.
         So maybe we get down a –
               while, see how the night goes round,
            take it from there awhile.
                  It being soul. There being

a thin wild mercury.

Just take it as it comes. Bounce.

Morning come to a country

everyone is talking 'bout.

May break away. Bring the south

ern thunder north; the mojo

creep, deep in the night. Alright.

FOR MERITORIOUS SERVICE
TO THE CAUSE OF MARVELDOM

May uh   lime bomb gone off a
sun⁄skittled dandelion wylde
                'tween sparkles
          & everything
                    what grisly hymnals shucks
                bluet gospels
      the pavement's   undulations went on
forever what seamed the
                          loneliest music yet achieved
                & wha la
            lavender apple orchard night

feel me squeal in my
pickscrape gliss
                yr windless mystic dejected Blakes blaringly
          pioneers reach
                    for the nearest   perhaps

      genital America
      yr strychnine please

AZALEAS BLOOMIN' WILD

Roman candle wars. Mountain
  erotic. House of sparrows.
& when we mob, we mob deep
    flaxen in the gloaming. Be
  nice. To what song did you most
      enjoy dancing? April rust.
When warm stars are dreamiest.

    Motorhead on vinyl. The
& of that. Otherwise post
red sounds. Trance pockets. New
      trampled jazz appliances.
  Big yesterday. Truth advance.
  Voice splice. Preface of Myrtles.
Quiet's billowy cadence.

        Grow your sails in the absence
  of long desired stillness.
  Unhand me. Country jug. March
      & hurry. Evening vervain.
        Let me ride. Creep shining bright.
  A⁄hush in those other years.
      I'll choke you when I'm sober.

        Spectacular meteor
      shower over the desert

expanse; a big band during
wartime; hornet on crocus.
Textbook pleasures. What would we
be without ice or birds? Dow
futures rose to start the day.

It's in the country that we
remember the steps to our
waltz. Lemon surge. Deep yellow
trumpet. Paper college. Sweet.
Wild center. Estate tea.
Momentum counts for a lot.
Some wet snowflakes possible

in higher elevations.
We hold hands, but don't say grace.
We're a tough little city.
I worry, collecting some
dust & feeling sorry.
Lay my head on your lap, stare
up at the sky till I fall

asleep, or pretend to. My
futurist dreams leave me so
    noisy, drinking a Diet
Coke by the ocean. In this
    version the liberators
    are greeted w/ flowers. Hit
        me as hard as you can, please.

Review. Sad & stunningly
    beautiful, those ballads. Don't
hold off. Light the pipes. Long green
    days spent bent at the desk. Song.
The endless grey of early
        spring stretches on endlessly.
    Pardon the traitors. Leave them.

    & when we mob, we mob deep.
I'd jump into the river
    Hudson, but it looks like rain.
When you fish in strange places
    you never know what you'll catch.
    Inside source at the Bingo
        Hall says Honky Tonk Man got

        a new gig. Throw water on
        the stone. Michael's writing a
            letter to the President.
        When the pretty girl touched me

I saw a light. Rose out of
my body. Thinking of my
favorite colors made me

smile. A summer night in
            the woods no one understands.
        It's too early in the film
for a ballad. Let me ride.

DAY SURGERY

got a corner on   lonesome monopolies
         new mown lawns so pepper
        psalm of salty repent & razors a tense sleetfall
          some tall yarn from yr time at Yale
        teaspoon repeater   storytellers best anemone
      yr perpetual coming of age soundtrack
sound champions set to roar
      always Septembers
     looseleaf metronome
   hard at work on my solipsism
       picking wildflowers by the airstrip
o blissful emeritus   panorama
    of melancholy   more terminal
in the rain   yr jacket a yellow piano
      slight amnesia but a blister
    the balloons nettlesome
     in sunbeam
      so beat fear & dreams out of my amplifiers
        embarrassment blueprint
         plentiful rationales
       baseline to baseline barefoot
          on the fearsome frontier of illusion
     so digital hardcore this meantime
     so immutable
       a pure moment of   nimble blame glitched
   although on any given day

our rolls could just as easily be reversed

    ok everyone   lets try the victory pyramid

ANOTHER AMAZÉD DWARF
ON SQUIRREL APPRECIATION DAY

insult jockeyed w/
the lonesome already &
yr Monday morning flight   squealed
into the television flush
of yr formerly golden sofa existence

the orange once
the pasture's promise   at dusk
my crush⁄harsher's drowsy drunk
stayed low &
slow to call out

alone in yr scratch ticket glamour
I've heard the several versions of the sin
the plentiful inequities

the pennant falling
in the water

JUST ANOTHER EMPIRE OF BRUISES
TO THE BIG SHOTS OF SCIENCE

the enchantress heartbreak foundation calls
all the firebase
carnations in flower
codename: decathlon
yr crosstalk deflector shy

rub out the tidal soul
a sulky thanks & hey tough it out

her botany felt drafty &
dirt-track raffle-winners take the cake
blurry besides baffled &

the Christmas present chemistry set made everyone nervous
complete w/ attack boos

suburban propane cold medicine frontiers
the recession orchestras current obsession
ghost of fundraiser heartbeat flashbacks

couldn't stomach the seasons wooden construction

MEMORY WIRE

so the memory standoff
couldn't account for the weather
emoticon folklore established
& the tropicana skyline compulsive
my keyless fugue aggressive in its demolition disputes
winters steroid throttle

my mistress she's a psilocybin symphony among the
Hawthorne
my galaxy dancer my Venezuela by moonlight

I'm penny guitars
for microwave starlings

I'm penny guitars
unflinching

& the mountain animation
required more of the color trials
for a thousand airsoft Vienna's
a kelly green sky grows wider w/each kiss

AN AMATUERS FAITHFULL OBSERVATIONS
OF A VARIABLE STAR

Previously your couch was on that wall.
Put the flowers away, the ginseng chicken
Is delicious. What did I see today?
Death eating a cheese burrito. One person
Talking to another. I was watching
Them put it down; they were really feeling
Each other. It's like when you're playing trombone
& think of a tomato. The door cracked
& I let God in. I pulled out the bay leaf.
Can you help me put it back in? & by
Evening we'll see a rightening in the sky.
It reminds me of the 70's when
We were free of the birds, & later,
The graffiti & broken soda machines
Of hip-hop; we built the house but couldn't
Avoid the curse. Those are lovely curtains.
That's what they say, a band of clouds.
& the elders dance & showoff their tattoos.
I only went back to see if they were still
Where I left them, the satanics of wondrous
Currents. Heart of palm, look me up
When you are through playing w/ the seasons.

SUBURBAN PROPANE

Enow of this silence. Of
the years adrift in the slade.
Sullenly wandering for
a home. Grave serious. Carp
again. I was living the
life. I was in a room w/
a group of people dancing.

Behind the door of hornets
that sweet & golden chord. Sound.
Assay, defend. Means refuse.
Ballet about the caboose.
Use the brilliantine to yr
Advantage, attack out of
The sun. I can finish w/

both hands. Whereof
the swollen sped to slacken.
I was living the again.
AOR mornings, Corporate
Rock afternoons, some Urban
in the evenings. Fuck it, lets.
Try heart. Just make it funky.

Someone's blowing me up. Wait.
Hushed, though w/ syllables crisp.
I could just make out. Summer
comes to the woods no one could
understand. I am sudden
a⁄weary, & sad. My slow
comfort, a bulb of words tuned

to quiver. I'll go dirty
blue. Blanked on that part about
setting the bike on fire.
Sweet Villa America
days, my kith & kin.
Play the piano real loud.
Tender perennial, push.

Purl. Poseidon⁄wide blue sky.
I came here to reinvent
myself, & still I carry
the jar of names through these streets.
Deep, steady my limp. Bright in
the distance. Sound years. I hope
I don't lose points
for not remembering.

IT'S NOW OR NEVER

Satan listened to your heart glowing
Before you even knew it glowed
 — John Coletti, "It's a Substitute for Thinking"

Shine deep. Emerge emblematic from the roar.
Come w/ the hurt; shaken, cooed a wounded
Mellow seldom, austere in the autumn raw.
O'er clouded mountains, word of a new féte rousted
Us from our title search, I could smell concrete.
All up in your business, as the always tied —
Off. I was open to new methods of discrete
Sequencing, or not so discrete. We got tight
Ousted from the darkening, & somehow thou
Mightn't consider crystal this clotted diction.
Just, this once. Equally, glitch, click & crow.
For a certain kind of blue hokum I did listen
To then Sprechstimme, a contour I could become
A new music to take w/ me after the summerlong.

Suppose these red meadows, absent sparrows.
I indwelt on the engines of why, ardent
In my woo, how then shall we take the tempo
Argue across the mights of someday, arrant
Wylde & crude? By this bare truth, engulft
& granted no stay against the against, against this goodbye.
I watched the world end one night in Brooklyn.
Popular anger. Why love is a lie
The lonely tell themselves to keep going. & the Safeway
Supermarket in the rain. Outside, the kites.
On yr cell you texted a desperate mayday
Mayday, calling in a favor of this starlight tonight.
Don't argue with me – it gets better, I told you.
Everything I ever told you about was untrue.

Enjoy the side-effects, strange as they may
Be, submit all the while to the tides timeless
Fanfare, cobbing together our ever hurrying days
Beneath the banners of Cockaigne, the tiger
In retrograde above us. We've got a bleeder
Here, a long gone brainbell jangler, all grit.
Painted portrait of the heart as compound fracture.
I've tried to grow a butterfly, go legit
Blossom, fruit, & die. Couldn't make it. A rare
Beyond, dreamt of & starless. & but when
Bleating bells chime the misfit hours of elsewhere
The corn will be swelling in the ear again.
My skies controlled by thought alone, distill
The weather. Sunwet hills in the distant, stippled.

When the bright lights no longer enchant, how lame
The midway spinning w/ its carousels
Must seem. I retreated to a place where the flame
Won't reach, this loudest pastoral's leveling decibels.
Ever called, in my grief I began to swan.
The fix is in. To care again is a dare
To fine pass on by. Forge me the emoticon
For broken, call me a cheat for healing. My nightmare
Come near to me. In circles we draft
In smoke & cocktails, that's dope so badass
Wheels spinning all the while. Cue the laughed.
Hear the words I chose to make the pain go away because
The lies I'm willing to tell to serve the conceit
— always fresh & full of bittersweet.

Friend me tonight, smush me under the hum.
I'm in the system, & I was hurt, redshirted
Like nothing you've ever seen, ever dumb
w/ volume. I'm still holding on. Wrong alert
Went up. Solid is my creep. Drum out thy
Wet wreckage, & under the brined spring sky chase
The last bright red coats against the snow, leave no alibis.
We might could get arbitrary, embrace
The rum capricious, voyage into our damage.
Daylight savings starts next week, she yawned
To the boy who'd gone to college in the village.
Refill the cups for another game of beer pong.
Volunteer for the helpline, pantomime the why
Delay the punchline, add more hurt to the turbine.

The essence remains the same, an aspect
Of the superstition still lingers anywhere
Peasant madrigals are sung. Love's subject
Rendered bare, no single edge left unspared.
Cheap & natural, it was wiser to go native
& groove. The captive, in his downtime
answered the latest meme in girlish cursive.
More adept songbirds took up the minor theme.
Relationship status: it's complicated.
Let me draw you in crayon – best parts
Last. Accompanied by a long essay.
Note the detail to the Technicolor heart.
Describe your ideal sound in one sentence.
Light sky & its blue reflection in the water.

Turn up the glint. Blazing in the break, want
Won't uh rescue you. Here. Lets start w/ distortion
& erasure; unique in the howling campaign
A wooden music from a wooden instrument.
Stark consolations of the northing oriole
Aside. We are seeing lines across the sky.
Uncertain how to notate this late winter squall's
Grandeur, or the shakeup in the cracker aisle
Over the whole schmear, I just don't translate
Well. My heroic suddenness unrelenting
& numb. & so it was I began to elaborate
Why the churn of attention is disquieting.
Answer don't jive w/ me or uh the mirror.
Any old darkness will do to take the measure.

Awestruck amongst the lilac havoc, struck
Dumb & thundered by this pale pink symphony
& every other voice you ever gave me come unstuck.
If I could only go back, make the necessary
Tweaks. Yet I can't bring myself to say farewell
Now that I've arrived in this new hell, unmourned.
I'd have it no other way. Dead, my cell
By the bed. Couldn't get my worlds aligned
In time, & late on sin's whirlwind arrived
Sparkled for the migration. Meet me on Hart
St., meet me, let's see how far we can drive
Into our dark history before the effort
To not not look back becomes too much. Await
My signal. Notate the sky. Then, detonate.

PERFECT TENDER RULE

For Nora

I.

A brief description of yr legendary status
would include rascality in the rough & tumble world,
assumption of the risk & thus sunken meadows.
Good eyes, tiger. The most pressing need now
is keeping the bridges in good repair. I still smelled
like pussy & saltwater; the way we danced cheek to cheek
slowly to the lightning out over the sea; unlike
the other animals unable to draw sadness in around us.
Unlimited, the minutes. We are lucky; between the fox
& the stars, pleading in the alternative.
If there was ever an adventure, it began here.

A touch thready, lovely autumn flecks of brown –
distant, that other world. But then, I always thought so.

What I found in the mountains was a picture
of a world where human emotion is trivial.

& w/o method those moments remained entirely
indistinguishable. Because it's observational it can't be tested.

But the data supports the hypothesis. I'm on hold, even today.
Three chords, my beating heart, if you hit it hard

enough. The days are shorter already.
I'll paint whatever is broken.

Skittish to begin w/ — first the secret, then the dots.
This is the country. There are no wolves here.

Where before there was only confusion, clearness & continuity
was restored simply by changing a letter here & there. I
deleted several lines while waiting for you to arrive. Song comes,
ownerless. It's not enough to just learn about terror. Suppose we
eventually reached the dream of pure empty comedy, what then?
or, or you love some other more than me; dazzled as I was
by the phenomena of accent, I pictured a violin in sound, full
on bird⁄twitch. I tell everyone I'm writing a novel; shirts vs. skins.
While you shut yr eyes to the everywhere glory according to my heart
expecting no other sign of approval sans the perfect clarity
of meaningless words carelessly spoken, describing the innocent enough
enigma of concern. By this intangible, we slack into our potential,
late maybe, but of no concern to the visual order of the new
American folklore, the little models of tedium — lists —
you can work backwards from that understanding; & after all
it's identifying the key moment & delivering it, matters most.

II.

As the acceleration continues
I only remember parts, I was in the woods
maybe still subscribing to the idea
of possession, what doctors recommend
most for headaches. I was watching
Zombie Apocalypse so incredibly high
& borrowing against the tradition. 13, the number
of the sun's death month, my harvest corn doll; last night
I, so selfish, forgot to tuck yr feet in
to keep the Mummy away; in my daydream
it happened this way: Mock king, sun spasm, game-face.
The nonstop astonishment option
pulled the string once again.
Froot Loops yr lips like, almost strawberry
frozen yogurt; surprisingly
enough I find myself
writing this in the evening.

O how I dreamt of you in life during the stutter.

Whereas the false alarm in the hawthorn
nullified my ability to vamp, the idea
& its kinetics ranged wide in the havoc of an as yet.
W/ candescence & excuse. Allegedly
bluebells by the oodles glitz the dooryard.

III.

Meanwhile, back in the jungle:
it was on & cracking

more than my heart
could ever take

the bluebird pennant
in earthquake light gone bonkers. Broken,

told ya. Perspective in the white
can play tricks on your mind.

I'm over this place. Totally.
But thanks for putting me onto

these easy mountain nights.
When can I open my eyes? Big panic,

tattooed my morning blue.
In the gun room the silver needs

polishing. Song the breeze,
boogie around the house

ass over tea-kettle. Watch your feet,
don't step in the bucket. It couldn't be argued

it was summer broke us.
Can I get real w/ you for just a second?

Have you gotten heavy lately?
Alternate north, you are so the furthest thing

from a waste of my time. Believe me.
We are intruders here, & the lions know it.

IV.

Sing to let the others know our position,
A tipping sparrow in the distance.

Enough already w/ the sky. It was a tickling deep
Inside that would work it's way out.

If everything works out as planned
We'll escape the horror of the village.

Yum, yum yellow. Summer. Open. House.
Proof, if you like. Pretty words, nice stories.

I put my head back to stop the bleeding.
You have what you wanna believe & that's all.

The kind of dream you spend the rest
Of the night trying to get back to.

Anyways too impatient for the predicted gorgeous
Tomorrow to come, to sleep. The vibe is key.

Before long the current will shift, the calm
Will be on, beneath yon cobalt vault.

Answers – I'm not the right person to ask them of.
It ain't the dipping, it's the counting that gets me.

44 LILACS

song of pine⁄winds haunts
    moon⁄views from the Capital
night grows autumn⁄late
    my October sweater on
        petals fell while & scattered
            sad, I watched things
thoughts   clear   awe
thrushes⁄like & we moaned

windy Cambridge fall
day   sparrow hops on brick
walk the Times
Weekend Arts open
    on her lap

            soup
            salad
            sandwiches

            glass
            plastic
            cans

locked mountain bike
to No Parking Anytime sign
my first dawn over
the Charles
        too much coffee
      gives me the shits
           fuck, no Wi-Fi

heard the ocean I
I heard nothing   hold my sleeve
cross the night   w/ me
of broken, freed from tides, free
past my window cloud wisps drift
not as it seemed
     chill   tear-dew
longing, unbearable

I lie on my belly
wet   fall   lawn
            reading a book
& you thought I was empty
    heard at a faintly distance
in autumn wind the
            I feel sorry dozing off
        said nothing is while

the puzzle mentioned
between the fox & the stars
adjusts in telling
moonlight   her shoulders   the dunes

        blue frost crisped bare harvest stalks
        very autumn
        out today
        w/ water on both sides

at this moment more
surer than I've ever been
about anything
because you   are   what I want

growing w/, like decibels
limoncello
              morning   sun
so ridiculous much

somewhere in the rush
somewhere into the rainbow

love you, w/ my fists
Massachusetts Avenue
stars above Arlington Heights
message erased
see   you   soon
as always blush & awe

on the other hand
only ideas are ideas
as in devotion
as in autumn, as in love
or the association
of morning   you
    dressing there
    before dawn, yr hair – up

waiting for the bus
autumn from summer came fast
time these days so strange

        Komatsu bucket loader
        Massachusetts Avenue
        construction work
        continues

        faster now, colds approach

dusk is so lonely
   through grey cloud light lemons, breaks
& makes me wonder
     is it love that's enough

bought at the market right now:
   cucumbers, greens
   for salad
tonight we'll be simple

in turning a turning
   a turning
     a turning both
toward & away
     a turning
between song
& thought   between silence
& idea   a turning
not from or
against but
w/ a turning   into
a turn because   & of

a turning despite
the respite
of a softest place's
tenderest touch – in
     spite of –

       – the first thing
          to go
          from the hurt
          was trust

sequentiality to idea
evidence or ephemerality

    as if understanding acceptance as a concept
    made dancing in the kitchen any different
    than dancing in the surf w/ you

    as if bleeding as a model
    never existed
    in the pursuit of deeper belief

44 lilacs
you told me was yr password
so I could get free
Wi-Fi at Starbucks today

while I waited for a job
& our new life
to begin
        — or was it *horizons*

ACKNOWLEDGEMENTS

Thanks, devotion, love to…

Chris Martin, Chris Rizzo, Ryan Murphy, Jess Mynes, John Coletti, Joseph Massey, Anselm Berrigan, CA Conrad, Mac Wellman, Lisa Jarnot, Louis Asekoff, Russell Dillon, Whit Griffin, Jason Myers, Michael Schiavo, Dustin Williamson, Andrew Mister, Paul Vargas, Aaron Tieger, Michael Carr, Matt & Katy Henriksen, Eric Unger, Evan Kennedy, Amber Nelson, Sharan Singh, Christopher Zubryd, Noah Hoffenberg…

to my Mom & Dad…

to Cedric, Matt, Jamie, & Danny…

to Jay MillAr, for whom I'm eternally grateful…

for Asa…

for Liam…

Poems in this collection have appeared in *Puppyflowers, Cannibal, Raleigh Quarterly,* & *Forklift, Ohio.*

COLOPHON

Manufactured in an edition of 500 copies in early 2010 by BookThug | Distributed in Canada by the Literary Press Group www.lpg.ca | Distributed in the United States by Small Press Distribution www.spdbooks.org | Shop on-line at www.bookthug.ca

BOOK
PRODUCTION
WAR ECONOMY
STANDARD

Type + design by Jay MillAr
Cover image by Stirling Prentice